Jesus
HEALED THEM ALL
&
ALL INCLUDES ME!

Jesus HEALED THEM ALL & ALL INCLUDES ME!

By
TRILBY R MCCLAMMY

XULON PRESS

Xulon Press
2301 Lucien Way #415
Maitland, FL 32751
407.339.4217
www.xulonpress.com

© 2020 by TRILBY R MCCLAMMY

All rights reserved solely by the author. The author guarantees all contents are original and do not infringe upon the legal rights of any other person or work. No part of this book may be reproduced in any form without the permission of the author. The views expressed in this book are not necessarily those of the publisher.

Unless otherwise indicated, Scripture quotations taken from the King James Version (KJV) –*public domain.*

Scripture quotations taken from the New King James Version (NKJV). Copyright © 1982 by Thomas Nelson, Inc. Used by permission. All rights reserved.

Scripture quotations taken from the Amplified Bible (AMP). Copyright © 1954, 1958, 1962, 1964, 1965, 1987 by The Lockman Foundation. Used by permission. All rights reserved.

Scripture quotations taken from the Holy Bible, New International Version (NIV). Copyright © 1973, 1978, 1984, 2011 by Biblica, Inc.™. Used by permission. All rights reserved.

Scripture quotations taken from the Holy Bible, New Living Translation (NLT). Copyright ©1996, 2004, 2007 by Tyndale House Foundation. Used by permission of Tyndale House Publishers, Inc.

Scripture quotations taken from New Life Version (NLV). Copyright © 1969 by Christian Literature International.

Scripture taken from The Passion Translation (TPT). Copyright © 2017 by Passion & Fire Ministries, Inc. Used by permission. All rights reserved. thePassionTranslation.com

Scripture quotations taken from the Good News Translation (GNT). Copyright © 1992 American Bible Society. Used by permission. All rights reserved.

Paperback ISBN-13: 978-1-6628-0349-9

Ebook ISBN-13: 978-1-6628-0350-5

DEDICATION

I dedicate this book to my sister, Melinda Hester, a mighty woman of God who has firsthand knowledge of Christ the Healer and His healing power. My sister was healed of breast cancer and continues to trust Jesus as her healer… Thanks for encouraging me to get this book completed. Love you much.

TABLE OF CONTENTS

DEDICATION v

ACKNOWLEDGEMENTS ix

CHAPTER 1 – JESUS HEALED THEM ALL 1

CHAPTER 2 – HELP ME BELIEVE 19

CHAPTER 3 – IF YOU CAN BELIEVE 27

CHAPTER 4 – BELIEVE WHAT? 35

CHAPTER 5 – EVERY WHIT WHOLE 45

CHAPTER 6 – MY TESTIMONY 59

NOTES 69

PRAYER FOR SALVATION 71

ABOUT THE AUTHOR 73

ACKNOWLEDGEMENTS

To my Father in heaven, my Lord and Savior Jesus Christ, and my ever-present help, the Holy Spirit – I am nothing and can do nothing without you. All glory, honor, and praise to You!

To my husband, Toney, who has walked this faith journey with me for over thirty years. I thank God that I was blessed to marry the "perfect" man for the ministry and work the Lord has chosen me to complete. Forever appreciated and loved!

To my New Covenant United Holy Church family – even though I consider myself a student of the Word of God, you forced me to study more than I care to sometimes. Thanks! Love you much!

Thanks again for the 2019 trip to Israel. I was able to stand in the places where some of the healings in this book took place. Forever grateful.

To my faithful "assistant," Carolyn Tillman: Thanks for reading a draft of this book and sharing your feedback. You are so appreciated.

To my partner in ministry, Minister Warren Alston: Thank you for combing through the book draft, section by section, offering your "scriptural expertise" so I can get this work finished.

ISAIAH 53:5

But He *was* wounded for our transgressions,

He was bruised for our iniquities;

The chastisement for our peace *was* upon Him,

And **by His stripes we ARE healed.**

1 PETER 2:24

who Himself bore our sins in His own body on the tree,

that we, having died to sins,

might live for righteousness—

by whose stripes you WERE healed.

If we were healed, then we are healed.

If we are healed, then

I AM HEALED!

Chapter One

JESUS HEALED THEM ALL

The four Gospels in the New Testament, written by Matthew, Mark, Luke, and John, are given by the inspiration of the Holy Spirit and record numerous healings and deliverances of individuals with different physical and mental sicknesses and diseases. These gospel accounts record individuals who came to Jesus themselves, those who were brought to Jesus by others, and some who came to Jesus on behalf of a family member or friend, as well as men and women who received healing simply because Jesus showed up in town. Jesus touched some and some touched Him. No matter the sickness or disease, or the length of time an individual had suffered, JESUS HEALED THEM ALL!

Everyone who came to Him in faith, who came believing He was able to heal and able to deliver, received their healing. There are a few accounts where Jesus had to help the person get in position to receive his or her healing. He would take the time and minister to the person first, and then he or she was positioned in faith to receive their healing or deliverance.

Thankfully, the Bible does NOT record Jesus turning anyone away. In fact, John 6:37 (NLV) says, *"I will never turn away anyone who comes to Me."* In Matthew 11:28 (NIV), Jesus actually bids all to come: *"Come to me, all you who are weary and burdened, and I will give you rest."* He did not discriminate based upon religion, ethnic background, social status, or type of sickness or disease. He HEALED THEM ALL!

The Bible also records where multitudes were brought to Him or followed after Him, and He healed them ALL. One person, two people, or large numbers of people – JESUS HEALED THEM ALL!

It is my prayer that these biblical accounts, taken from the New King James Version (unless stated otherwise), will provide proof to you that Jesus HEALED THEM ALL, and He can and will heal you too. I believe your faith will increase as you read these scriptures. I believe these words will work as medicine to your body and your soul, providing healing and deliverance for you. Let's make this confession at the start: **JESUS HEALED THEM ALL, AND ALL INCLUDES ME!**

➤ ACTS 10:38

*How God anointed Jesus of Nazareth with the Holy Spirit and with power, who went about **doing good and healing all** who were oppressed by the devil, for God was with Him.*

ACTS 10:38 (AMPC)

How God anointed and consecrated Jesus of Nazareth with the Holy Spirit and with strength and ability and power; how He went about doing good and, in particular, curing all who were harassed and oppressed by the power of the devil, for God was with Him.

In Acts, chapter 10, Peter was sent by the Spirit of God to Cornelius's house to preach the gospel. Cornelius was a centurion (military officer), of what was called the Italian Regiment from Caesarea. Up to this time, the gospel had been preached to the Jews only and now was, as commissioned by Jesus, being taken to the Gentiles. The Bible records that Cornelius was a devout and God-fearing man who gave generously to those in need and prayed to God always.

Peter preached a life-changing message to all those present in Cornelius's house. He declared to those in attendance that Jesus went about doing good and HEALING ALL that were oppressed by the power of the devil. He informed them that he was a witness of all the things, which Jesus did both in the land of the Jews and in Jerusalem (Acts 10:39). Peter was an eyewitness to Jesus healing everyone that came to Him.

➢ MATTHEW 8:16-17

> *When evening had come, they brought to Him many who were demon-possessed. And He cast out the spirits with a word, and **healed all who were sick**, that it might be fulfilled which was spoken by Isaiah the prophet, saying: He Himself took our infirmities, and bore our sicknesses.*

This text lets us know that many were delivered who were bound by evil spirits and Jesus healed all who were sick. The New Living Translation (NLT) of Matthew 8:17 says, *"This fulfilled the word of the Lord through the prophet Isaiah, who said, '**He took our sicknesses and removed our diseases**.'"* Isaiah's prophesy is recorded in Isaiah 53:4-5:

Surely He has borne our griefs and carried our sorrows; yet we esteemed Him stricken, smitten by God, and afflicted. But He was wounded for our transgressions, He was bruised for our iniquities; the chastisement for our peace was upon Him, and by His stripes we are healed.

The Amplified Bible (AMPC) translates Isaiah 53:4-5:

Surely He has borne our griefs (sicknesses, weaknesses, and distresses) and carried our sorrows and pains [of punishment], yet we [ignorantly] considered Him stricken, smitten, and afflicted by God [as if with leprosy].But He was wounded for our transgressions, He was bruised for our guilt and iniquities; the chastisement [needful to obtain] peace and well-being for us was upon Him, and with the stripes [that wounded] Him we are healed and made whole.

➤ MATTHEW 4:23-24

And Jesus went about all Galilee, teaching in their synagogues, and preaching the gospel of the kingdom, and **healing all manner of sickness and all manner of disease** *among the people. And his fame went throughout all Syria: and they brought unto him* <u>all sick people</u> *that were taken with divers diseases and torments, and those which were possessed with devils, and those which were lunatick, and those that had the palsy; and* **he healed them.**

MATTHEW 4:23-24 (AMPC)

And He went about all Galilee, teaching in their synagogues and preaching the good news (Gospel) of the kingdom, **and healing every disease and every weakness and infirmity** *among the people. So the report of Him spread throughout all Syria, and* **they brought Him all** *who were sick, those afflicted with various diseases and torments, those under the power of demons, and epileptics, and paralyzed people, and* **He healed them***.*

Jesus went all over Galilee teaching, preaching, and healing all sickness and diseases among the people.

People all over Syria heard the reports of the sick being healed, and they brought everyone that was sick, diseased, and in bondage to Jesus; and He healed them ALL. Did you read that? They brought ALL the sick people, even those with epilepsy (seizure disorders) and those paralyzed throughout ALL Syria. It didn't matter how long they had been sick or what disease they had; Jesus healed them ALL.

➢ MATTHEW 9:35

Then Jesus went about all the cities and villages, teaching in their synagogues, preaching the gospel of the kingdom, and **healing every sickness and every disease among the people.**

➢ MATTHEW 12:15

But when Jesus knew it, he withdrew himself from thence: and <u>great multitudes</u> followed him, and **he healed them all.**

Jesus went to the synagogue on the Sabbath day, and the Pharisees were trying to find something to accuse Him with. They asked Him whether it was lawful to heal on the Sabbath day. Jesus told them if a man's sheep fell into a pit on the Sabbath day, the man would lay hold and lift it out. He stated a man was better or more valuable than sheep. He told the Pharisees it was lawful to do good on the Sabbath day and followed that statement up by healing a man in the synagogue who had a withered hand. The Pharisees left and had a meeting to find a way to destroy Jesus. For this reason, Jesus went away from there and large crowds of people followed Him, and He healed them ALL. (You can read this entire account in Matthew 12:1-15.)

➢ MATTHEW 14:14

> *And Jesus went forth, and saw a <u>great multitude</u>, and was moved with compassion toward them, and **he healed their sick**.*

Jesus had been notified that John the Baptist had been beheaded and the disciples had buried his body. Jesus departed by ship into a desert place to be alone, but the people heard where He was going, and they followed Him on foot. When Jesus saw the great crowd of people, He was "moved with compassion." Compassion is not just being concerned or having pity for someone, but doing something about the suffering. In this case Jesus, being moved with compassion, healed ALL that were sick.

➢ MATTHEW 15:30-31

> *And <u>great multitudes</u> came unto him, having with them those that were lame, blind, dumb, maimed, and many others, and cast them down at Jesus' feet; and* **he healed them:** *Insomuch that the multitude wondered, when they saw the dumb to speak, the maimed to be whole, the lame to walk, and the blind to see: and they glorified the God of Israel.*

MATTHEW 15:30 (NLV)

> *Many people came to Him. They brought with them those who were not able to walk. They brought those who were not able to see. They brought those who were not able to hear or speak and many others. Then they put them at the feet of Jesus and* **He healed them**.

This scripture is a great faith-booster! Praise God! Large crowds showed up and brought those that were crippled or had suffered an injury, and those who were blind, deaf, and dumb, and Jesus healed every one of them. There was not one person sent away who still needed to be healed. There was not one person told to come back later, come back tomorrow, or told to meet Jesus at the next healing meeting. He healed EVERY ONE of them, and they praised and glorified God. He is the same yesterday, today, and forevermore (Heb. 13:8).

➢ MATTHEW 19:2

*And <u>great multitudes</u> followed him; and **he healed them there**.*

Jesus departed from Galilee and traveled to the coasts of Judaea, and the crowds of people continued to follow Him; and He continued to heal all those who came to be healed.

➢ MATTHEW 21:14

*And the blind and the lame came to him in the temple; and **he healed them**.*

These healings took place in the temple, after Jesus had gone in and chased away all those that were selling and buying in the temple. He turned over the tables of the money-changers and knocked over the seats of those that sold doves. He was upset the "house of prayer" had been turned into a "den of thieves" (see verses 12-13). However, even then, He still did not turn anyone seeking healing away. The blind and lame came to Him, and He healed them ALL.

➢ LUKE 6:17-19

> *And he came down with them, and stood in the plain, and the company of his disciples, and a <u>great multitude of people</u> out of all Judaea and Jerusalem, and from the sea coast of Tyre and Sidon, which came to hear him, and to be healed of their diseases;*
>
> *And they that were vexed with unclean spirits: and **they were healed**.*
>
> *And the whole multitude sought to touch him: for there went virtue out of him, and **healed them all**.*

LUKE 6:17-19 (NLT)

> *When they came down from the mountain, the disciples stood with Jesus on a large, level area, surrounded by many of his followers*

and by the crowds. There were people from all over Judea and from Jerusalem and from as far north as the seacoasts of Tyre and Sidon.

They had come to hear him and to be healed of their diseases; and those troubled by evil spirits were healed.

*Everyone tried to touch him, because healing power went out from him, and **he healed everyone**.*

People from all over Judea, Jerusalem, Tyre, and Sidon came to hear Jesus teach and preach, and to be healed of their sicknesses and diseases. It's so amazing the healing power was in such great manifestation that it was flowing from Him and everyone that touched Him was healed. Again, Jesus healed them ALL!

➢ LUKE 9:10-11

And the apostles, when they had returned, told Him all that they had done. Then He took them and went aside privately into a deserted place belonging to the city called Bethsaida.

*And the <u>people</u>, when they knew it, followed him: and he received them, and spake unto them of the kingdom of God, and **healed them that had need of healing.***

LUKE 9:10-11 (NLT)

When the apostles returned, they told Jesus everything they had done. Then he slipped quietly away with them toward the town of Bethsaida. But the crowds found out where he was going, and they followed him. He welcomed them and taught them about the Kingdom of God, and he healed those who were sick.

Jesus's twelve disciples had walked with Him, listened to Him preach, and watched Him heal and deliver multitudes. Luke records, in chapter 9, that Jesus authorized and instructed His disciples to go and do the same. Verse 6 of that chapter says, "*so they departed and went through the towns, preaching the gospel and healing everywhere.*" The disciples returned and told Jesus everything they had done.

Jesus took His disciples away to a desert place. He probably wanted to give them time to rest up, or time to get away so He could minister privately to them to build them back up. But the crowds of people found out where they were and followed them. Regardless of what Jesus's original plans were, verse 11 says He received or welcomed the people, talked with them about the kingdom of God, and healed EVERYONE who was sick. Isn't that good? Oh, how He loves!

➢ MARK 1:32-34

> *And at even, when the sun did set, they brought unto him <u>all</u> that were diseased, and them that were possessed with devils.*
>
> *And <u>all</u> the city was gathered together at the door.*
>
> *And he **healed many** that were sick of divers diseases, and cast out <u>many</u> devils; and suffered not the devils to speak, because they knew him.*

MARK 1:32-34 (Phillips Translation)

> *Late that evening, after sunset, they kept bringing to him all who were sick or troubled by evil spirits. The whole population of*

the town gathered round the doorway. And he healed great numbers of people who were suffering from various forms of disease. In many cases he expelled evil spirits; but he would not allow them to say a word, for they knew perfectly well who he was.

Jesus had just started in ministry, going around preaching and teaching in the synagogues, healing, and delivering people. Mark 1:28 says, *"His fame spread abroad throughout all the region round about Galilee."* He was now at Peter's house, probably for a meal and some rest after a long day. Peter's mother-in-law was laying down because of a great fever and since Jesus was there, they told Him about it. Mark 1:31 says, *"He came and took her by the hand and lifted her up, and immediately the fever left,"* and she started serving. Jesus healed fevers too!

That evening, the people kept bringing all who were sick or needed deliverance. Verse 33 says, *"all the city was gathered together at the door."* Jesus healed many, and many were delivered.

Note these verses say *"healed many"* and *"cast out many devils."* However, Luke, a beloved physician, records this same event in Luke 4:40: *"Now when the* sun was setting, <u>all they</u> that had any sick with divers diseases brought them unto him; and he laid his hands on <u>every one of them</u>, and **healed them**."

Luke writes the people took all those that were sick with many kinds of diseases, and Jesus laid hands on every one of them and **healed them ALL**.

➢ MARK 3:9-10

So He told His disciples that a small boat should be kept ready for Him because of the multitude, lest they should crush Him.

*For he had **healed many**; insomuch that they pressed upon him for to touch him, as <u>many</u> as had plagues.*

A great multitude followed Jesus from Galilee, Judaea, Jerusalem, Idumaea, and districts beyond Jordan because they had heard of the great things He had done and was doing. There were so many people that Jesus asked His disciples to get a boat ready so He wouldn't get crushed by the crowd trying to touch Him. He had already healed so many that these people came to Him to get their healing too.

Can you picture this scene? Verse eight called it a "great multitude." This could have been the same multitude that He fed with the two fish and five loaves. We know there were five thousand men on that day, plus women and children. It could have been at least fifteen thousand people pressing to touch Him. WOW!

JESUS HEALED THEM ALL, AND ALL INCLUDES ME! Shout that again–**Jesus healed them all, and all includes me!** That's good news. Believe it.!

First John 3:8 confirms that Jesus came to destroy the works of the devil (sin, sickness, disease, poverty, and death). For three and a half years, He walked the earth, teaching the Word to unbelievers and preaching the Gospel to the poor. He delivered the oppressed, the downtrodden, and the bruised (those that were hurt or injured). He freed those in captivity and saved all that were lost. He brought peace to the broken-hearted and cleansed the lepers. He healed the sick and the diseased. He made the blind to see, the deaf to hear, the lame to walk, and raised the dead back to life. Glory to God.

He is the same yesterday, today, and forever. He healed ALL that came to Him. I decree, "by His stripes you are healed, too"! Praise God. Jesus healed them ALL, and ALL includes ME.

Chapter Two

HELP ME BELIEVE

MARK 9:14-24

> *And when He came to the disciples, He saw a great multitude around them, and scribes disputing with them.*
>
> *Immediately, when they saw Him, all the people were greatly amazed, and running to Him, greeted Him.*
>
> *And He asked the scribes, "What are you discussing with them?"*
>
> *Then one of the crowd answered and said, "Teacher, I brought You my son, who has a mute spirit.*

And wherever it seizes him, it throws him down; he foams at the mouth, gnashes his teeth, and becomes rigid. So I spoke to Your disciples, that they should cast it out, but they could not."

He answered him and said, "O faithless generation, how long shall I be with you? How long shall I bear with you? Bring him to Me."

Then they brought him to Him. And when he saw Him, immediately the spirit convulsed him, and he fell on the ground and wallowed, foaming at the mouth.

So He asked his father, "How long has this been happening to him?" And he said, "From childhood.

And often he has thrown him both into the fire and into the water to destroy him. But if You can do anything, have compassion on us and help us."

Jesus said to him, "<u>If you can believe, all things are possible to him who believes</u>."

Immediately the father of the child cried out and said with tears, "<u>Lord, I believe; help my unbelief!</u>"

When Jesus saw that the people came running together, He rebuked the unclean spirit, saying to it, "Deaf and dumb spirit, I command you, come out of him and enter him no more!"

Then the spirit cried out, convulsed him greatly, and came out of him. And he became as one dead, so that many said, "He is dead."

But Jesus took him by the hand and lifted him up, and he arose.

Jesus, along with Peter, James, and John, was coming down from the mountain where the transfiguration had taken place (see verses 2-9) and found the other disciples being questioned by the scribes.

Jesus asked what they were questioning them about. One of the men in the crowd answered Him, telling Him that he had brought his son to them to cast out the mute spirit and they couldn't.

The boy was possessed by a spirit that had robbed him of his ability to speak. They brought the boy to Jesus. As they were bringing him to Jesus, he had an "attack" right in front of Jesus (verse 20). The father said to Jesus, *"if you can do anything, have pity on us and help us."* Jesus put the responsibility back on the father – *"if you can believe, all things are possible to him who believes."*

Basically, Jesus was saying, "It's not what I can do, but what you can believe." It's possible, if you believe. The man, crying, said, *"Lord, I believe; help my unbelief."*

I can picture the father crying hard, reaching out to Jesus with his hands clasped together in prayer, saying, "Lord, I do believe as best I can. Help me believe more."

Unbelief is defined as *"the state or quality of not believing."*[1] In other words, the man was telling Jesus that he believed in Him as the Healer, but he also had a belief in his son's evil condition. When you trust more on the natural things that you can see, hear, and/or feel, or negative circumstances, that is unbelief. When the man saw his son wallowing on the ground, foaming at the mouth, this produced unbelief. If you focus on the diagnosis or bad report received from the doctor or the pain in your body, this leads to unbelief. It's so easy to trust in the magnitude of the problem than the truth that Jesus is a healer, and He can and will heal you.

In the story above, Jesus completely delivered the man's son. The boy was healed from that very hour.

Matthew shares his version of this account in chapter 17:14-18. He adds a conversation that Jesus had with the disciples following the healing:

> *Then the disciples came to Jesus privately and said, "Why could we not cast it out?" So Jesus said to them, "Because of your unbelief; for assuredly, I say to you, if you have faith as a mustard seed, you will say to this mountain, 'Move from here to there,' and it will move; and nothing will be impossible for you."*

The disciples wanted to know why they couldn't deliver the man's son. They had been going around preaching, healing, and delivering others just like Jesus. They wanted to know what their problem was this time.

In private, He told them they could not cast out the spirit because of their unbelief or their lack of faith. He let them know if they had just a small amount of faith, as small as a mustard seed, they could speak to a mountain and it would move (verse 20). A mustard seed is a very tiny seed, the smallest of all seeds. It's like He was saying, if you had an inkling of faith, a spec of faith, just a tiny bit, nothing would be impossible to you. Apparently, the disciples were more focused on what they could see, hear, and feel at this time than the healing power that flowed from Jesus.

Mark 6 records that Jesus went back to His own country, Nazareth. While there, He was in the synagogue teaching and many who heard Him teaching and saw the mighty works He did were offended at Him. They couldn't see pass WHO they remembered Him to be growing up in Nazareth. Verse 3 records, *"Is this not the carpenter, the Son of Mary, and brother of James, Joses, Judas, and Simon? And are not His sisters here with us?"* Jesus wasn't able to do any mighty works in that city because of their unbelief. However, He did lay hands on a few sick people and healed them.

Mark 6:6 says Jesus, *"went round about the villages teaching."* His cure for unbelief was to teach. Why would teaching be the cure for unbelief? Romans 10:13 says, *"faith comes by hearing and hearing by the word of God."* Another translation says, *"So people believe because they hear. They hear because people tell them about Christ."*[2]

We are admonished in Proverbs 4:20-22 to pay attention to the Word and to keep it in our eyes and ears, for they are life and health to your body.

> *My son, pay attention to what I say; turn your ear to my words. Do not let them out of your sight, keep them within your heart; for they are life to those who find them and health to one's whole body.*

Joshua 1:8 tells us to meditate on the Word day and night to be prosperous and successful. Most people think finances when it comes to prospering, but prosperity includes the total man – spiritually, physically, and financially. Prospering physically involves being healed and whole; free from disease and pain; having a sound mind, as well as physical strength.

> *This Book of the Law shall not depart from your mouth, but you shall meditate in it day and night, that you may observe to do according to all that is written in it. For then you will make your way prosperous, and then you will have good success.*

You should spend time reading and listening to healing scriptures daily if possible. Practice meditating and memorizing healing scriptures as often as you can. The scriptures listed in chapter one is a good place to start reading over and over, meditating on them until they just flow out of your mouth. This will eliminate the unbelief and produce a trust in the power of Jesus to heal.

When Jesus started His ministry, Matthew 4:23 records He *"went about all Galilee, teaching in their synagogues, preaching the gospel of the kingdom, and healing all kinds of sickness and all kinds of disease among the people."* His teaching allowed people to trust in the power of God to heal. The Gospel of Christ is the power of God to salvation (health, deliverance) for everyone who believes.

Shout it out loud again: **"Jesus healed them all, and all includes ME!"**

Chapter Three

IF YOU CAN BELIEVE

MARK 9:23

> *"...If you can believe, all things are possible to him who believes."*

The key to doing anything or receiving anything is to *believe*. Jesus Himself said "all things are possible to him who believes."

Vines Expository Dictionary[2] defines *"believe"* as *"to be persuaded of, to place confidence in, to trust."* Merriam Webster dictionary[3] defines *"believe"* as *"to accept the word or evidence of."*

Everybody believes in something – right or wrong, good or bad, seen or unseen. It's easier to do than we think. There are those who work forty hours a week, believing they will receive a paycheck at the end of the week. We schedule appointments months in advance, believing there will be a tomorrow. We get behind the wheel of a car, not knowing how it works. We take off down the highway, sometimes in a new car, sometimes used, sometimes barely working; but nevertheless, we drive or ride. The Bible calls this believing or *FAITH* (to trust in, rely on, and depend upon).

John 3:16, the most recognized scripture in the world and translated in thousands of languages, reads *"For God so loved the world that He gave His only begotten Son, that whoever believes in Him should not perish but have everlasting life."* God sent Jesus to this world because He loved everyone and He did not want those in the world to live destructive lives – sick, broken, depressed, oppressed, weary or worn-out. Jesus came that we could enjoy life to the full (John 10:10).

The key to living this life is to BELIEVE. Believe in Jesus. Believe that He died on the cross and rose from the dead for your salvation. Matthew 11:19 tells us Jesus came to seek and to save the lost. The word "save" in this verse also means "heal and make whole."

Jesus told us in Mark 11:22, *"to have faith in God."* We are to trust in, rely on, and depend upon God. We must believe in and be persuaded of the fact that Jesus is the Healer and has provided healing for each of us.

A great example of faith can be found in the book of Mark, chapter 2, regarding the faith of five men who surely believed Jesus could heal the sick and cure the lame.

> *And again* He entered Capernaum after *some* days, and it was heard that *He was in the house.*
>
> *Immediately many gathered together, so that there was no longer room to receive them,* not even near the door. And He preached the word to them.
>
> **Then they came to Him, bringing a paralytic who was carried by four men.**
>
> **And when they could not come near Him because of the crowd, they uncovered the roof where He was. So when they had broken through, they let down the bed on which the paralytic was lying.**
>
> **When Jesus saw their faith, He said to the paralytic, "Son, your sins are forgiven you."**
>
> *And some of the scribes were sitting there and reasoning in their hearts,*

"Why does this Man speak blasphemies like this? Who can forgive sins but God alone?"

But immediately, when Jesus perceived in His spirit that they reasoned thus within themselves, He said to them, "Why do you reason about these things in your hearts?

Which is easier, to say to the paralytic, 'Your sins are forgiven you,' or to say, 'Arise, take up your bed and walk'?

But that you may know that the Son of Man has power on earth to forgive sins"—He said to the paralytic,

"I say to you, arise, take up your bed, and go to your house."

Immediately he arose, took up the bed, and went out in the presence of them all, *so that all were amazed and glorified God, saying, "We never saw anything like this!"*

Jesus was in His hometown, in a house where many had crowded in and around the door to hear Him preach the Word. Four men carrying a paralyzed man on a bed came to the house, but were not able to enter because of the crowd. They took the man up to the roof, broke off the roof, and lowered him down, possibly right where Jesus was teaching. Verse 5 says *"Jesus saw their faith."* He saw the great lengths they went through to get the paralyzed man to Him for healing. They tore the roof off someone else's house; that's bold faith, and it paid off. The man was delivered, and the people glorified God.

Another example of faith is found in Mark 5:22-24, 35-43 where Jairus, the ruler of the synagogue, came to Jesus because his little daughter was at the point of death. He came and fell at Jesus's feet, and asked Him to come and lay His hands on her that she may be healed and live. Jesus went with him, and a great multitude of people followed Him. While they were on their way to Jairus's house, some came from his house and told him his daughter was dead, and he didn't need to trouble Jesus any further.

Jairus had risked his reputation and his position in the synagogue by going to Jesus. He worked in the synagogue that Jesus frequented. I'm sure he had probably seen and/or heard about the people Jesus had healed. He may have heard about the widow woman whose son had been brought back from the dead during the funeral processional. (See Luke 7:12-17.)

Regardless of what Jairus had to lose in going to Jesus for help, He had come to believe Jesus was his daughter's only hope of living; and by faith, he went to Jesus for help, and now his servant told him she had died.

Verse 36 of Mark 5 says, *"As soon as Jesus heard the word that was spoken, He said to the ruler of the synagogue, 'Do not be afraid; only believe.'"* Can you picture this scene? Jesus walks over to Jairus, grabs him with both hands by his robe, looks him square in the eyes, and, with such great authority, says, *"DO NOT be afraid; ONLY believe!"* Glory to God; gives me chills just writing this.

I can imagine with those words from Jesus, Jairus took each step toward his house, encouraging himself and repeating those words to himself:

"Only believe. Only believe. Only believe."

"Keep the faith, Jairus. Do not be afraid. Only believe."

"Don't lose hope now. Keep on believing. All things are possible if I believe."

"He raised the widow's son; He will raise my daughter too. Only believe."

Jesus and Jairus finally made it to the house. He took Peter, James, and John in with Him. Mark 5:37-43 records:

And He permitted no one to follow Him except Peter, James, and John the brother of James.

Then He came to the house of the ruler of the synagogue, and saw a tumult and those who wept and wailed loudly.

When He came in, He said to them, "Why make this commotion and weep? The child is not dead, but sleeping."

And they ridiculed Him. But when He had put them all outside, He took the father and the mother of the child, and those who were with Him, *and entered where the child was lying.*

Then He took the child by the hand, and said to her, "Talitha, cumi," which is translated, "Little girl, I say to you, arise."

Immediately the girl arose and walked, for she was twelve years of age. And they were overcome with great amazement.

But He commanded them strictly that no one should know it, and said that something should be given her to eat.

Jairus had told Jesus in the beginning, "*Come and lay Your hands on her, that she may be healed, and she will live*" (verse 23). That's what he believed and all things are possible to him that believes. Jarius's daughter was healed and she lived.

Let's take a moment and, like Jairus, declare what you believe:

I BELIEVE GOD

I BELIEVE JESUS IS THE HEALER

I BELIEVE ALL THINGS ARE POSSIBLE TO ME

I BELIEVE JESUS HEALED THEM ALL, AND ALL INCLUDES ME

I ONLY BELIEVE

Chapter Four

BELIEVE WHAT?

MATTHEW 9:27-31

When Jesus departed from there, two blind men followed Him, crying out and saying, "Son of David, have mercy on us!"

And when He had come into the house, the blind men came to Him. And Jesus said to them, "<u>Do you believe that I am able to do this?</u>"

They said to Him, "Yes, Lord."

Then He touched their eyes, saying, "According to your faith let it be to you." And their eyes were opened. And Jesus

> *sternly warned them, saying, "See that no one knows it."*
>
> *But when they had departed, they spread the news about Him in all the country.*

Believe He Is Able To Heal

As I stated earlier, it's easy for us to believe. The problem is what and how we believe. To believe is just to have confidence in or to trust. Unfortunately, some people have more confidence in or trust in the sickness they have been diagnosed with, or the disease that has manifested in their bodies, than the healing power of Jesus. Which one do you spend more time talking about? What do you go around telling everybody about? The sickness or the Healer?

In the account above, these blind men followed Jesus, crying out for mercy. Jesus asked the blind men specifically if they believed He was *"able"* to do what they were asking, and they said yes.

The blind men had confidence in Jesus's ability. They believed Jesus was able to heal. He touched their eyes, and their eyes were opened. Jesus said, *"according to your faith"* or according to what you believe, "let it be to you." Jesus is **able** to heal you as well.

Isaiah 53 guarantees us that Jesus has borne our sicknesses, weaknesses, and distresses, and carried our sorrows and pains. He was chastised for our peace and well-being, and with the stripes that wounded Him, we were healed and made whole. God anointed Jesus with the Holy Ghost and power, and He went about doing good and HEALING ALL that were oppressed by the devil. No doubt, Jesus is ***able*** to heal.

Believe He Is Willing To Heal

The two blind men in the previous section believed Jesus was able to heal and they received their sight. They had confidence in Jesus's ability to heal and because of their faith, they received.

Mark records another healing account where we read about a man who believed in Jesus's ability to heal, but he wasn't quite sure if Jesus was "willing" to heal.

MARK 1:40-45

> *Now a leper came to Him, imploring Him, kneeling down to Him and saying to Him, "If You are willing, You can make me clean."*

Then Jesus, moved with compassion, stretched out His hand and touched him, and said to him, "<u>I am willing; be cleansed</u>."

As soon as He had spoken, immediately the leprosy left him, and he was cleansed.

And He strictly warned him and sent him away at once,

and said to him, "See that you say nothing to anyone; but go your way, show yourself to the priest, and offer for your cleansing those things which Moses commanded, as a testimony to them."

However, he went out and began to proclaim it freely, and to spread the matter, so that Jesus could no longer openly enter the city, but was outside in deserted places; and they came to Him from every direction.

Lepers had a skin disease and, depending on the severity of the disease, were classified unclean and had to dwell alone outside of the city. (See Leviticus 13:46.) This leper came to Jesus and was basically on his knees, begging Jesus to make him clean. He was confident in

Jesus's ability to heal him, but he wasn't so sure if Jesus would (*"If You are willing"*).

We can understand why he would have difficulty in knowing whether Jesus was willing to heal. He was an outcast who was forced to live alone, and no one could or would dare to touch him.

Ministers hear this a lot of times from sick people. They say, "I know Jesus can heal, but?" "I know Jesus is able to heal, but?" They question whether He WILL heal them. Often times, these questions of doubt are related to condemnation from sinful living, past sins, or wrong teaching. If the condition in a person's body is the result of sinful activities, such as drinking or drugs, they may think it is punishment or that they deserve what's happening in their bodies and Jesus may not be willing to heal them. Some are taught that Jesus healed in the Bible, but that's done away with; while others believe that Jesus heals some but not everybody, as if you have to meet some special qualifications. NO. NO. NO. Jesus provided healing for everybody. It's according to what you can believe, not how sweet or innocent you are.

Jesus is merciful and will not hold past, present, or future sins against anyone. He died for the sins of the whole world. Isaiah 43:25 (GNT) says, *"And yet, I am the God who forgives your sins, and I do this because of who*

I am. I will not hold your sins against you." Ephesians 1:7 (AMPC) says, *"In Him we have redemption (deliverance and salvation) through His blood, the remission (forgiveness) of our offenses (shortcomings and trespasses), in accordance with the riches and the generosity of His gracious favor."* He loves you and wants you healed and delivered from every sickness and every disease, regardless of how or why you become sick.

In the leper's account, Jesus was moved with compassion. Jesus's compassion is not just sympathy or pity; He was moved to do something about the situation. He reached out and touched this man and cleansed him. The leper was immediately healed of leprosy. Jesus has the ability to heal, and He is willing to heal ALL. Praise His name.

Luke 19:10 says, *"...for the Son of Man has come to seek and to save that which was lost."* The phrase "to save" in this scripture is also translated "to heal" or "to make whole." Jesus came to seek and to save, heal, and make whole. Jesus is WILLING to heal all that come to Him, and that includes YOU.

Believe His Word

Matthew 8:5-13

> *Now when Jesus had entered Capernaum, a centurion came to Him, pleading with Him,*
>
> *saying, "Lord, my servant is lying at home paralyzed, dreadfully tormented."*
>
> *And Jesus said to him, "I will come and heal him."*
>
> *The centurion answered and said, "Lord, I am not worthy that You should come under my roof. But only speak a word, and my servant will be healed.*
>
> *For I also am a man under authority, having soldiers under me. And I say to this one, 'Go,' and he goes; and to another, 'Come,' and he comes; and to my servant, 'Do this,' and he does it."*
>
> *When Jesus heard it, He marveled, and said to those who followed, "Assuredly, I say to you, I have not found such great faith, not even in Israel!*

And I say to you that many will come from east and west, and sit down with Abraham, Isaac, and Jacob in the kingdom of heaven.

But the sons of the kingdom will be cast out into outer darkness. There will be weeping and gnashing of teeth."

Then Jesus said to the centurion, "Go your way; and as you have believed, so let it be done for you." And his servant was healed that same hour.

In the scriptures above, a centurion came to Jesus, pleading with Him for his servant who was paralyzed and distressed with intense pain. Jesus told him He would come and heal him. Jesus doesn't turn anyone away who comes to Him for deliverance (Matt. 11:28).

However, the centurion didn't feel worthy enough for Jesus to come to his home. He asked Jesus to just speak the Word and his servant would be healed. He had an understanding of the authority of Jesus's words. He believed if Jesus just spoke a word, his servant would be healed. Jesus called that *"great faith."*

Isaiah 55:11 declares, *"So shall My word be that goes forth from My mouth; It shall not return to Me void, But it shall accomplish what I please, And it shall prosper in the thing for which I sent it."*

The NIV translation of this verse says, *"so is my word that goes out from my mouth: It will not return to me empty, but will accomplish what I desire and achieve the purpose for which I sent it.*

The Word of God produces or brings results when spoken and believed. God sent His Word and healed and delivered (Ps. 107:20).

He told the centurion He had not found anyone that had such faith — such a belief in the authority of His words. The servant was healed that same hour because the centurion believed. All things are possible to him that believes.

In John 4:46-50, a nobleman came to Jesus and asked Him to come and heal his son, who was dying. Jesus said to him, *"'Go your way; your son lives.' So the man **believed the word that Jesus spoke** to him, and he went his way"* (verse 50).

The scriptures say that as the nobleman was going his way, his servant met him and told him his son lived. He asked his servant what time did his son began to get better and he told him the time. It was at the same hour that Jesus had said, *"your son lives."* **If you can believe, all things are possible to him who believes**.

Jesus said heaven and earth would pass away, but His Word would never pass away (Matt. 24:35). Isaiah 40:8 says, *"The grass withers, the flower fades, But the word of our God stands forever."*

The Word of God is pure, right, and endures forever, and Jeremiah 1:12 says that God watches over His Word to perform it (fulfill, accomplish, or make sure it comes true). Numbers 23:19 records, *"God is not a man, that He should lie, Nor a son of man, that He should repent. Has He said, and will He not do? Or has He spoken, and will He not make it good?"* Believe the Word.

Jesus is able. Jesus is willing. Believe it. Jesus healed them all, and all includes me.

Chapter Five

EVERY WHIT WHOLE

JOHN 7:23 (KJV)

If a man on the sabbath day receive circumcision, that the law of Moses should not be broken; are ye angry at me, because I have made a man <u>every whit whole</u> on the sabbath day?

JOHN 7:23 (NKJV)

If a man receives circumcision on the Sabbath, so that the law of Moses should not be broken, are you angry with Me because I made a man completely well on the Sabbath?

There was a pool in Bethesda where a great multitude of invalids lay who were blind, crippled, and paralyzed, waiting for the moving of the water. The fifth chapter of the book of John records an angel going down at a certain season into the pool and troubled the water, and whosoever stepped in first after the water was troubled was made **whole** of whatsoever disease he had.

Jesus stopped by this pool one day and took notice of a man laying by the pool, who had been disabled for thirty-eight years. Jesus said to the man, **"Do you want to be made whole?"** You would think the man would scream, "YES! YES! YES! I DO!" However, he answered, *"Sir, I have no man to put me into the pool when the water is stirred up; but while I am coming, another steps down before me."*

What? Oh come on, man! This is Jesus – just say YES.

Thankfully Jesus, with His compassionate, patient, and loving self, said to the man, *"Rise, take up your bed and walk."* The man was ***immediately made whole***. He was no longer disabled, got up from his bed, and walked. Jesus heals ALL.

Remember the words Jesus speaks will not return void or empty, but will produce. In this case, His words produced healing. In John 6:63, Jesus said, *"The words that I speak to you are spirit, and they* are life." His spoken words will bring life to your body and your body parts.

How? By faith. By believing that Jesus is able, willing, and His Word is true.

By faith (believing the words Jesus spoke), the man had to get up, pick up his bed, and walk. He could have said, "but I'm disabled. I've been this way for thirty-eight years; how can I rise? How can I walk?" But the power in that spoken word brought forth immediate healing to the man. He got up from his bed and walked. He was made whole.

The dictionary[5] defines *"whole"* as:

1. free of wound or injury (unhurt)//
2. recovered from a wound or injury (restored)
3. being healed
4. free of defect or impairment (intact)
5. physically sound and healthy (free of disease or deformity)
6. mentally or emotionally sound
7. having all its proper parts or components (complete, unmodified)

The man was immediately made whole after being disabled for thirty-eight years. He was now physically sound and healthy, healed mentally and emotionally sound after suffering for so long.

Jesus made this man whole on the Sabbath day – the day of rest. The man was confronted by some Jewish men because he was walking and carrying his bed. He told them he was doing what he was told to do by the man that had made him well. He had no clue who Jesus was at the time.

Jesus found him later in the temple and declared to him, "*thou are made whole, sin no more.*" What glorious words. The man went back and told the Jewish men that Jesus was the one who had healed him.

Sadly, these men were upset with Jesus for healing a man on the Sabbath and wanted to kill him. How ridiculous is that? A man was healed and they were more concerned about the letter of the law. Jesus asked them, "*are ye angry at me, because I have made a man every whit whole on the sabbath day?*"

Every whit whole! That's so King James! Some probably would say, "every bit whole!" Hallelujah! However way you say it, the man was made whole. (You can read the whole account in chapters five and seven of the book of John.)

Jesus is still making men "*every whit whole*" today, and that includes you. All we need do is believe. Remember, all things are possible to him that believes.

Let's look at another account of someone being made whole. This happens to be one of my favorite accounts in Mark 5 (KJV).

And a certain woman, which had an issue of blood twelve years,

And had suffered many things of many physicians, and had spent all that she had, and was nothing bettered, but rather grew worse,

When she had heard of Jesus, came in the press behind, and touched his garment.

For she said, If I may touch but his clothes, I shall be whole.

And straightway the fountain of her blood was dried up; and she felt in her body that she was healed of that plague.

And Jesus, immediately knowing in himself that virtue had gone out of him, turned him about in the press, and said, Who touched my clothes?

And his disciples said unto him, Thou seest the multitude thronging thee, and sayest thou, Who touched me?

And he looked round about to see her that had done this thing.

But the woman fearing and trembling, knowing what was done in her, came and fell down before him, and told him all the truth.

And he said unto her, Daughter, <u>thy faith hath made thee whole</u>; go in peace, <u>and be whole of thy plague</u>.

This woman, who was not identified other than being a "certain woman," had a bleeding condition that had been going on for twelve years. She had spent all her money on treatments from many doctors, and nothing had helped; in fact, her condition had only grown worse.

But thanks be to God, the scriptures say, *"she had heard of Jesus."* Remember, *"faith comes by hearing"* (Rom. 10:17). She probably had sat in her window and heard different ones coming from the healing services talking about the multitudes of people whom Jesus had healed. She may have even had relatives stop by and yell up to her who were healed just by touching Him. Hope started building up. She started talking to herself, "If I just touch Him, I can be made whole." One day faith came and she acted on it. She got herself dressed and made her way to the healing meeting, telling herself, "If I may touch but his clothes, I shall be whole."

She got outside, and this multitude of people were passing by, being led by Jesus. As it turned out, they were headed to Jairus's house to heal his daughter. She started pressing her way to Jesus. This woman had been bleeding for twelve years. She probably was weak, sickly, and could barely walk. We also know that Jewish law declared her to be ceremonially unclean due to her bleeding issue. (See Leviticus 15:19-28.) According to the Levitical law, anything or anyone she touched became unclean as well. The fact that she was in the crowd, pressing her way to Jesus, means that each person who bumped into her would have become unclean too—including Jesus. But, after suffering for twelve years, surely she was in a critical position and desperate for a miracle. Matthew 9:20 records she "*came from behind and touched the hem of His garment.*"

When she touched His garment, the fountain of blood dried up and she felt in her body that she was healed. Jesus knew the healing power had gone out of Him, and

He turned around to see who had touched Him. The woman came and fell down before Him and told Him "all the truth." She probably told Him when the issue of blood started, how she had spent all her money with no cure, and probably how she had been stuck in the house for twelve long years with no visitors. This day, Jesus said to her, *"Daughter, thy faith hath made thee whole; go in peace, and be whole of thy plague."*

What a day of rejoicing! Jesus healed them all, and all includes me! Remember, He is the same yesterday, today, and forever. He changes not (Mal. 3:6). He is no respecter of persons (Acts 10:34). What He did for one, He will do for you. Amen.

Below are a few other accounts from the King James Version of the Gospels to increase your faith in the Word of God, and in the One who makes all whole.

➢ MARK 2:17

> *When Jesus heard it, he saith unto them,* ***They that are whole have no need of the physician, but they that are sick:*** *I came not to call the righteous, but sinners to repentance.*

➢ MATTHEW 14:35-36

And when the men of that place had knowledge of him, they sent out into all that country round about, and brought unto him all that were diseased;

*And besought him that they might only touch the hem of his garment: and as many as touched were made perfectly **whole**.*

[NOTE: These men may have been the ones the woman with the issue of blood heard had touched the hem of Jesus's garment and were made whole.]

➢ MATTHEW 15:21-28

Then Jesus went thence, and departed into the coasts of Tyre and Sidon.

And, behold, a woman of Canaan came out of the same coasts, and cried unto him, saying, Have mercy on me, O Lord, thou son of David; my daughter is grievously vexed with a devil.

But he answered her not a word. And his disciples came and besought him, saying, Send her away; for she crieth after us.

But he answered and said, I am not sent but unto the lost sheep of the house of Israel.

Then came she and worshipped him, saying, Lord, help me.

But he answered and said, It is not meet to take the children's bread, and to cast it to dogs.

And she said, Truth, Lord: yet the dogs eat of the crumbs which fall from their masters' table.

*Then Jesus answered and said unto her, O woman, great is thy faith: be it unto thee even as thou wilt. And her daughter was made **whole** from that very hour*

➢ MATTHEW 15:30-31

And great multitudes came unto him, having with them those that were lame, blind, dumb, maimed, and many others, and cast them down at Jesus' feet; and he healed them:

*Insomuch that the multitude wondered, when they saw the dumb to speak, the maimed to be **whole**, the lame to walk, and the blind to see: and they glorified the God of Israel.*

[NOTE: maimed = crippled, crooked, disabled, mutilated, injured, damaged]

➢ MARK 3:1-5

And he entered again into the synagogue; and there was a man there which had a withered hand.

And they watched him, whether he would heal him on the sabbath day; that they might accuse him.

And he saith unto the man which had the withered hand, Stand forth.

And he saith unto them, Is it lawful to do good on the sabbath days, or to do evil? to save life, or to kill? But they held their peace.

*And when he had looked round about on them with anger, being grieved for the hardness of their hearts, he saith unto the man, Stretch forth thine hand. And he stretched it out: and his hand was **restored whole** as the other.*

➢ MARK 6:56

*And whithersoever he entered, into villages, or cities, or country, they laid the sick in the streets, and besought him that they might touch if it were but the border of his garment: and as **many as touched him were made whole**.*

➢ MARK 10:46-52

And they came to Jericho: and as he went out of Jericho with his disciples and a great number of people, blind Bartimaeus, the son of Timaeus, sat by the highway side begging.

And when he heard that it was Jesus of Nazareth, he began to cry out, and say, Jesus, thou son of David, have mercy on me.

And many charged him that he should hold his peace: but he cried the more a great deal, Thou son of David, have mercy on me.

And Jesus stood still, and commanded him to be called. And they call the blind man, saying unto him, Be of good comfort, rise; he calleth thee.

And he, casting away his garment, rose, and came to Jesus.

And Jesus answered and said unto him, What wilt thou that I should do unto thee? The blind man said unto him, Lord, that I might receive my sight.

*And Jesus said unto him, Go thy way; thy faith hath made thee **whole**. And immediately he received his sight, and followed Jesus in the way.*

➢ LUKE 17:11-19

And it came to pass, as he went to Jerusalem, that he passed through the midst of Samaria and Galilee.

And as he entered into a certain village, there met him ten men that were lepers, which stood afar off:

And they lifted up their voices, and said, Jesus, Master, have mercy on us.

And when he saw them, he said unto them, Go shew yourselves unto the priests. And it came to pass, that, as they went, they were cleansed.

And one of them, when he saw that he was healed, turned back, and with a loud voice glorified God,

And fell down on his face at his feet, giving him thanks: and he was a Samaritan.

And Jesus answering said, Were there not ten cleansed? but where are the nine?

There are not found that returned to give glory to God, save this stranger.

And he said unto him, Arise, go thy way: **thy faith hath made thee whole.**

Chapter Six

MY TESTIMONY

I know you have heard someone exclaim, "if it ain't one thing, it's another," or "always going through something," or "every time I go to the doctor, it's always something." I don't recall actually saying those exact words out loud myself, but I definitely have had those thoughts. There was a time in my life I even disliked going to the doctor for a routine check-up, because it seem like they always had something negative to report.

My mom starting taking my sister and me for annual gynecological appointments as teenagers because of a "blood" disease that she was diagnosed with. Each time, it seemed like I always had abnormal exams and the physician would make some comment about "well, one out of so many women get this." I would always wonder, *Well why me? Why did I have to be the one?* Year after year, abnormal exams were followed by some outpatient surgical procedures. I was told I would probably have a hysterectomy by age thirty.

In 1988, I was introduced to the word of faith and found out that healing belongs to me, and I didn't have to be sick anymore or suffer abnormalities in my body anymore. Growing up, I always loved reading the New Testament and the stories in the Old Testament, but didn't know much about my rights and privileges as a believer (most of these are found in the Epistles from the book of Romans to Jude.)

But thanks be unto God for sending me to a church where the full gospel was being preached and taught. I found out that as a born-again believer, a Christian, Jesus had already provided forgiveness of sin, healing and wholeness, prosperity, soundness of mind, peace, joy, protection, and eternal life for whosoever would believe and receive it.

In 1990, following the birth of my second child, I received a report of an abnormal exam. Because of my past records, the doctor wanted me to undergo a surgical procedure that would require me undergoing anesthesia. He scheduled a follow-up appointment before scheduling the procedure. Good for me; I took that time to get back on my healing scriptures – confessing and believing those truths. Again, the Word worked. I didn't have to undergo that procedure and for years my exams were normal; and at age fifty-six, I still have not had a hysterectomy and I do not plan on having one as long as Jesus is my healer.

I will say that I had some strange follow-up visits. I was asked by several different physicians if anyone ever talked to me about the possibility of having leukemia, sickle cell anemia, or lupus. I started having thoughts that the doctors were trying to make me sick. These were not simple diagnoses either; these things were serious. What in the world!

In April 1996, I preached my initial sermon on the first healing service of the year at my church. The title of my message was *"Do You Believe I Am Able to Do This?"* My message was taken from Matthew 9:27-30, from the account of the two blind men who followed Jesus crying, asking Him to have mercy on them. I started my sermon that evening giving my personal testimony of healing. I must admit that this was the first time my family members heard about the suffering I had been enduring. I wasn't trying to hide it or anything like that. I just believe if you believe the Word of God, you should act like it's true. The Word said I was healed. I believed I was healed and I acted like I was healed! You don't go around telling everybody everything the doctors say, or talking about how bad you feel. I declared my healing every time somebody asked me the question, "How you doing?" My response was, "I am healed, thank you! How are you?" Or "I am well; how are you?"

For months prior to preaching that evening, I had been suffering physically in my body. Ironically, I had just completed a healing brochure for a friend who was passing them out whenever he went to the hospital for dialysis treatment and other appointments. I reread and studied all the healing scriptures and healing stories in the Old and New Testaments so that I could type up a healing brochure for him. Thankfully, I was filling my heart up on the healing truth, unknowingly preparing myself for a faith fight.

Shortly after finishing this brochure, I started having some pain in my arms. It seemed like a vein in my arm would swell in one area, and it would hurt severely. I was having almost unbearable pain in my thumb and, at the time, I was a medical transcriptionist. I typed some days up to seven hours, and typing made it worse. I was told by a physician that the pain in my arm was inflammation, and the thumb pain could be related to some form of arthritis. He wanted to schedule me for a formal exam so he could give me some medication to help with the inflammation and the pain.

However, I am not very fond of taking pills, so I declined the prescription from the doctor. He said if it got worse, he would run some tests and I could start treatment. I agreed to that. I ended up wrapping my thumb with tape when it would hurt to type, which helped some. I just endured the swelling pain in my arm. Unfortunately, the pain worsened and I even started experiencing swelling in my face.

I remember walking into the doctor's office having to follow up on some abnormal bloodwork. The doctor had reviewed my records and concluded that because of previous issues and questionable diagnoses that this episode could possibly be cancer. She asked me to go ahead and get undressed for the exam.

When she walked out of the door, I declared out loud, "with His stripes, I am healed!" I must admit, as I undressed, I noticed my body had broken out in a sweat reacting to the words it heard from the doctor. I repeated, "with His stripes, I am healed!" this time to my body. The doctor came in, completed the exam, and scheduled more tests.

Weeks later, I received the test results in the mail, and they basically confirmed that something was going on in my body. I read the report and I heard the words, "WHOSE REPORT WILL YOU BELIEVE"?

I declared, "I believe the report of the Lord. His report says I AM HEALED!"

My husband read the report and asked what I was going to do. I told him the doctor's report would catch up with the Lord's report. I put the letter back in the envelope and made my faith stand on THE HEALING WORD and POWER of God.

I worked in a hospital, and sometimes symptoms were noticeable. The doctors in my office were concerned and wanted me to start some medication, but I had decided to trust the Word of God and use it as my medicine. I read and confessed healing scriptures day and night, according to Proverbs 4:20-22 – *"My son, give attention to my words; Incline your ear to my sayings. Do not let them depart from your eyes; Keep them in the midst of your heart; For they are* life to those who find *them, And health to all their flesh."* Another translation of verse 22 says, *"For they are* life unto those that find them and ***medicine*** *to all their flesh."*[6]

I must admit I had some really bad days and nights. One night, the pain was so bad, I got up from my bed and went into another bedroom so I wouldn't alarm my husband. I knew if I told him, he would take me to the emergency room. At one point during that night, the pain was so bad I couldn't move and I couldn't call out to my

My Testimony

husband in the other room. I couldn't quote scriptures either. I could only silently meditate them. That night, I wanted to go to the hospital, but I couldn't even get up. I was in so much pain. I concluded that if I died, it would be okay. I knew I would wake up looking into the face of my Lord and Savior, Jesus Christ.

I think I passed out either from the pain or sheer exhaustion. The alarm went off the next morning. By then, I was able to get up, get dressed, and get my kids to school. Afterward, I stopped by one of the minister's house from my church. I went in, asked for prayer, they prayed, and I went to work. HEALED PEOPLE ACT LIKE IT! Weeping endures for a night, joy definitely comes in the morning (Ps. 30:5).

A few days later, I received a phone call from one of the deacons from my church. He asked me, how was I doing? I said, "Fine.' He said he didn't want any faith talk. He wanted to know how I was "really doing." Again, I said I am "really fine. I am well, I am healed in Jesus's name!" He didn't like my answer, but it was the truth. I believe the Word of the Lord, and I wasn't going to say anything contrary to it. That next morning (Sunday), that same deacon was getting ready to pray over the offering and he looked at me, called my name, and declared, *"The Lord said, you shall live and not die and declare the works of the Lord.*" I smiled, told the Lord "thank you," and starting searching my Bible for that scripture. Psalm 118:17 –"*I shall not die, but live, And declare the works of the LORD.*"

I stood on that truth and I can testify the WORD WORKS, and the WORD HEALS. I started looking and feeling normal long before the doctor's report changed. But eventually those test results caught up with the Lord's report and every test came back normal. Hallelujah. Jesus healed them all, and all included ME.

I shared my testimony that evening at that healing service and reported to those in attendance that I was completely healed.

I studied the healing scriptures, the healing stories in the Gospels, and read faith books on healing. I stood on the healing scriptures, confessed the word regularly (sometimes daily for months at a time), and believed that "by His stripes I was healed; Jesus bore pain in His body so I didn't have to endure pain in mine and God would satisfy me with a long life."[7] Praise God. The Word worked.

Psalm 107:20 says, "*He sent His Word and healed them.*" It produced in my life.[8]

This is my testimony. I am not advocating for anyone to stop taking medicine or to refuse medication. You do what's necessary to sustain life. Listen to the doctors, take the medication until the Lord or the doctor takes you off. HEALING always comes! Trust in the Lord! Believe in His healing power and His healing Word!

JESUS HEALED THEM ALL, AND ALL INCLUDES ME! BELIEVE IT!

Shout it with me one more time:

JESUS HEALED THEM ALL, AND ALL INCLUDES ME!

NOTES

1. Dictionary.Com Unabridged. Based on the Random House Unabridged Dictionary, © Random House, Inc. 2020

2. Worldwide English (New Testament) (WE) © 1969, 1971, 1996, 1998 by SOON Educational Publications

3. "Believe." *Merriam-Webster.com Dictionary*, Merriam-Webster, https://www.merriam-webster.com/dictionary/believe. Accessed 3 Nov. 2020.

4. Vine, W. "Belief, Believe, Believers–Vine's Expository Dictionary of New Testament Words." Blue Letter Bible. Last Modified 24 Jun, 1996. https://www.blueletterbible.org/search/dictionary/viewtopic.cfm

5. "Whole." *Merriam-Webster.com Dictionary*, Merriam-Webster, https://www.merriam-webster.com/dictionary/whole. Accessed 3 Nov. 2020.

6. Jubilee Bible 2000 (JUB), Copyright © 2013, 2020 by Ransom Press International.

7. First Peter 2:24; Matthew 8:17; Psalm 91:16.

8. Isaiah 55:11.

PRAYER FOR SALVATION

Dear Reader,

If you have never made Jesus the Lord of your life, this is a perfect opportunity. God so loved the world that He sent His only begotten on to save the world. His on came into the world that we could have and enjoy life. He died and shed His blood on the cross for our sins. He rose again on the third day so that we could live life eternally. He is seated now on the right hand of the Father, praying for us. Make Him your Savior today. It will be the best decision of your life.

Let's pray:

Dear God in heaven,

You said in Your Word, Romans 10:9-10, that if I confess with my mouth the Lord Jesus, and shall believe in my heart that God raised Jesus from the dead, I shall be saved. I believe with my heart that Jesus died on the cross for my sake and has risen from the dead. I repent of my sins and I renounce the past.

Jesus, come into my heart, be the Lord of my life. I receive forgiveness. I receive salvation. I receive your Holy Spirit. I receive eternal life. Thank you, Lord Jesus.

I will trust and follow You as my Lord and Savior. Guide my life and help me to do Your will.

I thank you for saving me.

Sign _____

Date _____

Welcome to the Family!

I pray God's richest blessing abound in your life spiritually, physically, and financially in Jesus's name!

Be blessed!

Min. Trilby

ABOUT THE AUTHOR

Trilby McClammy has been in the ministry faithfully serving the Lord for twenty-four years. She is the co-founder of Love & Power Ministry, a ministry dedicated to breaking the bondage of religion and tradition off the minds of people and bring healing and deliverance to people through the preaching and teaching of the Gospel of Jesus Christ. She is the youth pastor at New Covenant United Holy Church in Durham, North Carolina, where she also serves as the superintendent of Christian education.

Trilby has published a book titled, "The Sky is Always Blue," which has been a blessing and encouragement to many around the world. She is happily married to Toney McClammy and has three children, Chanelle, Danielle, and Toney Jr.; a son-in-law, Chris Dixon; a godson, Rodriquez Turrentine; and four beautiful grandchildren.

www.ingramcontent.com/pod-product-compliance
Ingram Content Group UK Ltd.
Pitfield, Milton Keynes, MK11 3LW, UK
UKHW022221230426
12048UKWH00016BA/980